ACCORDING TO MY WILL, I DID EAT

On Original Sin

BISHOP RAPHAEL

Translated by
St. Mary and St. Moses Abbey

According to My Will, I Did Eat: On Original Sin
By Bishop Raphael

Translated from Arabic by St. Mary & St. Moses Abbey.

Copyright © 2024 Coptic Orthodox Diocese of the Southern U.S.A.

All rights reserved.

Designed & Published by:
St. Mary & St. Moses Abbey Press
101 S Vista Dr., Sandia, TX 78383
stmabbeypress.com

All Scripture quotations in the footnotes of this book, unless otherwise indicated, are taken from the New King James Version® Copyright © 1982 by Thomas Nelson, Inc. Used by permission. All rights reserved.

Contents

About the Cover Icon	v
Forward	vii

CHAPTER ONE
Introduction — 11

CHAPTER TWO
How Do We Understand Our Faith? — 13

CHAPTER THREE
The Sources of the Teaching of the Church — 22

CHAPTER FOUR
The Issue of the Sin of our Father Adam — 37

About the Cover Icon

In the middle of the icon, our father Adam is standing beside our mother Eve who appears with her head bowed. Sorrow fills her countenance, and she is lifting both of her hands in an attempt to cover her face out of regret and shame, which sin always causes. Behind her appears the tree of the knowledge of good and evil, and around its branches that serpent of old is twisted, staring at them with hatred and pride. Our father Adam appears holding the fruit which caused his fall and the fall of all humankind in him. For we are all the children of Adam, and from him and in him, and this meaning is embodied in drawing human faces on his body. For we are truly from his loins and have inherited sin from him, as the Church teaches us through the Fathers of the Church.

While the left side of the icon is painted with dark colors, representing death which entered into the world through the envy of the devil, we find on the right side of the icon vivid, exhilarating colors.

On the right side, the hand of our good Savior appears, pierced in redemption for us, holding our father Adam's hand, that He may lift him up from the mire of sin and make him dwell in the prepared kingdom. It was inevitable that we recall the Golgotha scene, in which the power of death was annulled.

Therefore, the icon represents all the stages: beginning with darkness, evil, death, and regret, to end with light, righteousness, resurrection, and joy.

Forward

This book came at the right time! For erroneous teachings have circulated among the youth, contrary to that which we have received from the Holy Scriptures, the saintly Fathers, and all who have taught us throughout history, speaking of the ancestral sin of our father Adam and our mother Eve in an erroneous way. And they make inquiry concerning some of the holy doctrines and teachings in a manner which harbors skepticism and aggression, drawing from the modern era!

For we have received this faith from:

1. The Fathers, with a high aptitude, who studied and searched the Holy Scriptures.
2. [Those who] recorded the sayings of the saintly Early Fathers: St. Athanasius, St. Cyril, And St. Dioscorus.
3. Also the fathers of our time: Pope Kyrillos IV, Pope Kyrillos V, Pope Kyrillos VI, Pope Shenouda III, and Pope Tawadros II.

4. The recent holy councils and the sayings of the saintly Fathers.

In this book, His Grace Bishop Raphael answers the following critical questions, based on the Holy Scriptures and the sayings of the [Early] Fathers:

✤ How do we understand our faith?

✤ What are the sources of the teaching of the Church?

✤ What about the sin of our father Adam?

✤ What is the meaning of the sentence of excommunication by the Church?

✤ [Were we] created and did we sin in Adam—in Adam and not with him?

✤ [What is the meaning of] "the likeness of sinful flesh"?

✤ [Is there] a biological, genetic aspect of sin?

✤ [What is the meaning of] in Christ we are justified by grace?

✤ What about infants? Why do we baptize them?

✤ What is the summary of the Christian faith?

All these treasures are contained in one book, and the one who asks for more will find them in the writings of the [Early] Fathers, H.H. Pope Shenouda III, H.H. Pope Tawadros II, and the bishops, priests, deacons of the Church, each with his specialty.

Forward

May the Lord bless these pages for the readers, and may He reward His Grace Bishop Raphael for his fruitful, concentrated effort in teaching and preserving the Orthodox faith.

Through the prayers of our beloved shepherd, His Holiness Pope Tawadros II, and the honorable metropolitans and bishops of the Church, may the grace of the Lord be upon us all.

Bishop Moussa

General Bishop for Youth Affairs

1

Introduction

Several theological, interpretational problems were stirred up in the Church, preoccupying many of the youth and [church] servants, which led to a sort of discord, skepticism and finger-pointing. Many have requested the declaration of the Church's opinion on these nuanced theological issues.

Because I consider myself a friend of many on both sides of the ideological conflict, and have had ample discussions with both sides, I have discovered common points in understanding on some of the raised issues.

The [main] Christian principle is preserving love toward all, for love is the distinguishing mark of a Christian. "A new commandment I give to you, that you love one another; as I have loved you, that you also love one another. By this all will know that you are My disciples, if you have love for one another."[1] Even if we disagreed on opinions and interpretations, our adherence to the faith should not be a kind of fanaticism, nor of hatred of the other, nor of contempt of the other's opinions and faith; "but God has shown me that I should not call any man common or unclean."[2]

Therefore, I have taken it upon myself to attempt the role of ideological reconciliation, to preserve the peace of the Church and the soundness of teaching, "redeeming the time, because the days are evil."[3]

"Walk in wisdom toward those who are outside, redeeming the time. Let your speech always be with grace, seasoned with salt, that you may know how you ought to answer each one."[4]

I would like to make mention, at the beginning of this book, that what is included in it of quotes and information is the outcome of the effort of many loved ones, who volunteered—thanks be to them—to search for the Fathers' texts from Greek, English, and Arabic sources (translated by others), and they wished for their names not to be acknowledged, for the sake of the heavenly reward. May the Almighty God reward them and repay them for their labor and godly zeal.

---

1 John 13:34–35.
2 Acts 10:28.
3 Ephesians 5:16.
4 Colossians 4:5–6.

2

How Do We Understand Our Faith?

Do we discover our faith?

We are not going to discover our faith again, nor do we need to hold new councils to put in place new definitions[5] of the faith. Our faith is immovable, "for the faith which was once for all delivered to the saints."[6] The Coptic Orthodox Church has preserved the faith it received from the Lord, which St. Mark the Evangelist preached and the fathers preserved, in godliness, spirituality, and the fear of God, throughout the generations.

St. Athanasius the Apostolic says:

---

5   Also: specifications.
6   Jude 1:3.

Let us also examine the tradition, teaching, and faith of the Catholic Church from the beginning, which is nothing other than what the Lord gave, and the Apostles preached, and the Fathers preserved. On this the Church is founded, and whoever falls away from it can no longer be nor be called a Christian.[7]

Despite the clarity of the Christian faith and its simplicity, people may sometimes disagree on the interpretation of some of the items of this great, salvific faith.

Why do They Disagree?

The passage of Christianity throughout twenty-one centuries, naturally led to the accumulation of many theological experiences in interpretation on the level of the churches of the whole world. Many theories appeared in history explaining the Christian faith, and the matter became very complicated, which is of interest to no one except the specialized scholar who analyzes every idea and is able to follow its author and the evolution of the idea and its impact on the Christian thought in general. The schools of thought have become interwoven, and you find

---

7 Athanasius the Great and Didymus the Blind, *Works on the Spirit*, M. DelCogliano, A. Radde-Gallwitz, and L. Ayres, trans. (Yonkers, NY: SVS Press, 2011), 96.

yourself standing before a whirlpool of ideas[8] whose origin you do not know nor to whom they belong.

Note that "doctrine and faith" are not [the same as] "the interpretation and explanation of the doctrine." For all Christians believe in the incarnation, redemption, and the divinity of the Lord Christ, but may disagree on the explanation of these matters of the faith.

Everyone Thinks They Possess the Truth

Each interpretational idea of the faith has its own luster, philosophy, proofs, defenders and supporters. And it may be an idea that is sound in some of its parts, or it may have some truth. And the mind may be enamored with it because of how logical it is, and there may be unanimity on it by the scholars, which would inspire that this idea of the faith is genuine and Patristic, expressing the Orthodox faith in its roots. [All of this] makes the person incapable of distinguishing between what is true and false.

Do Hades and Hell Exist?

For example, there is an idea that the good God did not create Hades. Hades is rather a mere psychological state the sinner is in, as a result of their separation from God. This idea is nice, logical, after one's own heart, harbors some truth, and is

---

8   Also: thoughts.

comforting when responding to the skepticism of atheists concerning the goodness of God, His fatherhood, His love, etc.

Nevertheless, the question is, "Is this the thought [or understanding] declared in the Holy Scriptures? Is this the teaching of the esteemed Fathers, [which they agreed upon] unanimously? Is this what we pray with in the liturgical services?"

So What is the Solution?

Therefore, it is necessary at the present time that we go back to the simplicity of the faith declared in the Holy Scriptures, which was explained by the Early Fathers, in purity and unanimity. And what is more important is that they prayed with it in the liturgical services[9]. Even if people agreed on an interpretation or an explanation of a doctrine in a particular way, what we care foremost about is the view of our Coptic Orthodox Church, as the ancient Fathers said it unanimously, and as they declared it in their interpretations and their liturgical prayers.

We do not take lightly the opinions of the wise, prudent, and the scholarly, whose studies and research we truly learn from, but [only] from that which is in agreement with what we have received and learned from the Holy Scriptures and the interpretations of the [Early] Fathers. "Do not

---

9   "Liturgical services" is literally "liturgies."

remove the ancient landmark which your fathers have set."[10]

We are likewise committed, foremost, to that which we [use to] speak to God, in our liturgical prayers, far removed from the theories and interpretations of the scholars and the prudent. Let them search and discover the meanings as they see [fit], and let us pray, in the innocence of children, with what we have received from our Fathers, of liturgical prayers, in the Divine Liturgy, the Psalmody, the Agpeya, and others. For it would be neither reasonable nor faithful, that I teach from the pulpit what is contrary to that with which I speak to God, before the altar and in [my] room.

> As I urged you when I went into Macedonia—remain in Ephesus that you may charge some that they teach no other doctrine, nor give heed to fables and endless genealogies, which cause disputes rather than godly edification which is in faith. Now the purpose of the commandment is love from a pure heart, from a good conscience, and from sincere faith, from which some, having strayed, have turned aside to idle talk, desiring to be teachers of the law, understanding neither what they say nor the things which they affirm.[11]

---

10 Proverbs 22:28.
11 1 Timothy 1:3–7.

Why are we Preoccupied with These Issues?

As some have come out, trying to sow doubts in what we have received from our faithful Fathers, this places upon all [of us] the responsibility of searching in the treasures of the [Early] Fathers, with a faithful and pure spirit, unaffected by the thoughts of others; that we may be filled with the richness of the Fathers' interpretations, in light of the Holy Scriptures, the Coptic liturgies, the Fathers who are considered pillars, and the canons of the ecumenical Councils which are affirmed by our glorious Church. To this end, we are not moved by our private convictions, but by faithfulness to the faith and the Fathers, and what we daily pray with in our rich liturgies.

> But avoid foolish disputes, genealogies, contentions, and strivings about the law; for they are unprofitable and useless. Reject a divisive man after the first and second admonition, knowing that such a person is warped and sinning, being self-condemned.[12]

The Constancy of the Faith

These, which the catholic[13] Church decided upon in the ecumenical Councils, are definitions[14] of

---

12 Titus 3:9–11.
13 That is, universal.
14 Literally: specifications.

the faith, which cannot be doubted, even though there may be other theological opinions by some Fathers. For it is known that the esteemed Church Fathers did not agree on some theological opinions, but each saintly [Church] Father had his own theological perspective and his own character[15] in comprehending the one divine truth; nevertheless, they did not accuse each other of having deviated from the faith or of having fallen into heresy. But they stipulated unanimity in opinion, that it [i.e. the opinion] may be worthy for the Church to adopt, through which the Church may transmit the teaching to [future] generations, in faithfulness, far from [any] private desire.

The Difference Between Doctrine and Theology, and Between the Faith, Opinion, and Heresy

There is a vast difference between a doctrine and the explanation of the doctrine. For though the doctrine is as firm as granite, we may disagree on the explanation [of the doctrine].

Therefore, there is also a difference between the faith of the catholic [i.e. universal] Church and the personal opinion of some Fathers. The personal opinion remains a mere opinion which is respected, but it does not express the faith of the catholic Church.

---

15 Literally: flavor.

And if there were a personal opinion that represented a danger to the theology of salvation, it would be utterly rejected as innovation or heresy.

"Hold fast the pattern of sound words which you have heard from me, in faith and love which are in Christ Jesus. That good thing which was committed to you, keep by the Holy Spirit who dwells in us."[16]

"Hold fast what you have, that no one may take your crown."[17]

The Contemporary Theological Conflict

Now we return to the subject of our study on the contemporary theological conflicts, which have recently been raised in the Church, [though] uncalled-for.

The topics of the contention are many and divergent. You could easily, however, discover the beginning of the thread, because an error, by necessity, leads to an error, and so the chain of errors continues, linked and connected. Had it been left like this, the whole of the Christian faith would have deviated into extremely strange currents, away from the mind of our Lord Jesus Christ.

Therefore, the most important role of a bishop in the Church is "holding fast the faithful word as he has been taught, that he may be able, by sound

---

16   2 Timothy 1:13–14.
17   Revelation 3:11.

doctrine, both to exhort and convict those who contradict."[18]

Between the Understanding and the Terms

There may be similarity in thought between the two groups of the theological dialogue, with disagreement on the use of expressions. Let us, however, remember a principle professed by the Early Fathers, that if we agreed on the understanding, there would be no problem with the words which we use to express the one Divine truth.

Nevertheless, we must adhere to the expressions which are settled upon in the Church, especially in our liturgical prayers, along with an explanation of the meaning contained in these expressions, to eliminate any misunderstanding or any ambiguity. We must adhere to [the principle of] not changing what has been settled upon in the Church, of concepts, expressions, and terms; and that all of us should have a single thought and a single expression, according to the Church, and not according to our [own] convictions and feelings; nor that our expression should be according to the laws of reason and intellect, rather than according to the Holy Scriptures, the [Church] Fathers, and the liturgies.

"But if anyone seems to be contentious, we have no such custom, nor do the churches of God."[19]

---

18 Titus 1:9.
19 1 Corinthians 11:16.

3

The Sources of the Teaching of the Church

We should, in all these, return to the sources of teaching in the Church, and these are, in order: The Scriptures, the explanations of the Fathers in unanimity, the liturgies, and the local and ecumenical Councils which are recognized by our Church.

1. The Holy Scriptures

The Holy Scriptures are the uppermost guardian of all the teaching in the Church, for it is the first, uppermost, and principal source of the divine revelation. The Fathers exerted all their effort and life to interpret them, and not with [a sense of] superiority over it, of course. For [any] teaching that is contrary to any text of the Holy Scriptures is not permitted.

> And that from childhood you have known the Holy Scriptures, which are able to make you wise for salvation through faith which is in Christ Jesus. All Scripture is given by inspiration of God, and is profitable for doctrine, for reproof, for correction, for instruction in righteousness, that the man of God may be complete, thoroughly equipped for every good work.[20]

St. Irenaeus says:

> [We] being most properly assured that the Scriptures are indeed perfect, since they were spoken by the Word of God and His Spirit; but we, inasmuch as we are inferior to, and later in existence than, the Word of God and His Spirit, are on that very account destitute of the knowledge of His mysteries.[21]

St. Athanasius the Apostolic also says, "For the tokens of truth are more exact as drawn from Scripture, than from other sources."[22]

St. John Chrysostom says, "In the holy

---

20 2 Timothy 3:15–17.

21 Irenaeus *Against Heresies*. In *Ante-Nicene Fathers* 1, P. Schaff, ed. (Peabody, MA: Hendrickson Publishers, 2012), 399.

22 Athanasius *Defense of the Nicene Definition*. In *Nicene and Post-Nicene Fathers: Second Series* 4, P. Schaff, ed. (Peabody, MA: Hendrickson Publishers, 2012), 172 (henceforth cited as NPNF²).

Scriptures it is impossible without loss to pass by one jot or one tittle, we must search into all. For they all are uttered by the Holy Spirit, and nothing useless is written in them."[23]

> And so we have the prophetic word confirmed, which you do well to heed as a light that shines in a dark place, until the day dawns and the morning star rises in your hearts; knowing this first, that no prophecy of Scripture is of any private interpretation, for prophecy never came by the will of man, but holy men of God spoke as they were moved by the Holy Spirit.[24]

"The law of the Lord is perfect, converting the soul; the testimony of the Lord is sure, making wise the simple."[25]

2. The Church Fathers

These are the Fathers who contributed to explaining and formulating the faith. The condition for accepting their opinion is that there must be unanimity in the Church on this opinion.

How Should we Read [the Works of] the Fathers?

---

23 John Chrysostom *Homilies on St. John* 36.1 (NPNF[1] 14:125).
24 2 Peter 1:19–21.
25 Psalms 19:7.

Some may agree with us concerning what we believe in, and yet others of the beloved scholarly may disagree. Each group relies on the sayings of the Fathers and serious, respected studies which deserve that we consider them with esteem. For there is no absolute truth, except in God Himself; and no opinion is devoid of some truth. Also the different opinions may be complementary, if we considered them with the eye of concord, and not with the eye of clashing, lying in wait, and disdain.

All that we desire and wish for is the attainment of mutual understanding on the faith issues which are currently disagreed upon, without losing love and the peace of the Church. "Let all that you do be done with love."[26]

"Now the fruit of righteousness is sown in peace by those who make peace."[27]

Therefore, let us agree upon some principles for reading the teachings of the Fathers.

Principles for Reading the [Writings of the] Fathers

1. We should read the texts of the Fathers in their original language or [read] faithful, reliable translations. "And the things that you have heard from me among many witnesses, commit these to

---

26 1 Corinthians 16:14.
27 James 3:18.

faithful men who will be able to teach others also."[28]

Saint Athanasius the Apostolic says:

> Let us also examine the tradition, teaching, and faith of the Catholic Church from the beginning, which is nothing other than what the Lord gave, and the Apostles preached, and the Fathers preserved. On this the Church is founded, and whoever falls away from it can no longer be nor be called a Christian.[29]

2. We should read the Patristic studies done by researchers and scholars who are faithful to the spirit of the Church and Her faith. We should also always have the spirit of discernment and discretion, lest others' thoughts lead us into intellectual labyrinths, far removed from what the Fathers intended in their writings. "And know His will, and approve the things that are excellent, being instructed out of the law."[30]

3. We should read [the writings of] the Fathers who are considered pillars in the Church, and who contributed, in a faithful way, to explaining and formulating the faith. For not every ancient writing the Church has authorized.

---

28 2 Timothy 2:2.

29 Athanasius the Great and Didymus the Blind, *Works on the Spirit*, M. DelCogliano, A. Radde-Gallwitz, and L. Ayres, trans. (Yonkers, NY: SVS Press, 2011), 96.

30 Romans 2:18.

> Thus says the Lord: "Stand in the ways and see, and ask for the old paths, where the good way is, and walk in it; then you will find rest for your souls. But they said, 'We will not walk in it.'"[31]

St. Cyril the Pillar of the Faith advises [us] to read particular books of interpretation, saying:

> I think that those who are engaged with the Holy Scriptures need to approach all writings that might be good, noble and free from harm. In this way, by gathering what many people have observed from various points of view about the same thing, and by bringing them all to bear on one point, they will climb to a good measure of knowledge. They will imitate the bee, a wise worker, and build the sweet honeycomb of the Spirit.[32]

4. We should be cautious about taking the opinions and conclusions of scholars as handed-down [truths], which are not up for discussion. For scholars themselves disagree [with each other] on their conclusions. "These were more fair-minded than those in Thessalonica, in that they received the word with all readiness, and searched the Scriptures

---

31 Jeremiah 6:16.
32 Cyril of Alexandria, *Commentary on John* 1, J.C. Elowsky, T.C. Oden, and G.L. Bray, eds.; D.R. Maxwell, trans. (Downers Grove, IL: IVP Academic, 2015), 5.

daily to find out whether these things were so."[33]

5. Reading and studying should be [done] with a faithful spirit, not influenced[34] by previous thoughts or by people we love. Neither should we reject a thought [i.e. an opinion] merely because it was said by someone we do not accept or whose teaching we reject. Reading also should be [done] unhurriedly, and with understanding and meditation, comparing texts to each other, to achieve a holistic view. "You search the Scriptures, for in them you think you have eternal life; and these are they which testify of Me."[35]

6. We should read [the writings] of the Fathers in general, and not of one of them only, because the Divine truth cannot be restricted to one [Church] Father; therefore, unanimity in the Church on an opinion or thought is a [critical] condition, so that it [i.e. the opinion] may suffice to be a teaching the Church adopts. "It seemed good to us, being assembled with one accord, to send chosen men to you with our beloved Barnabas and Paul."[36]

St. Cyril the Great says:

Well, we think the same things about the economy of our Savior as the holy Fathers did before us. We regulate our own minds by

---

33 Acts 17:11.
34 Literally: directed.
35 John 5:39.
36 Acts 15:25.

reading their works so as to follow in their footsteps and introduce nothing that is new into the orthodox teachings.[37]

7. We should read the thought of the Father as a whole, without interruption, so that we may understand his intention and the current of his teaching. As there is danger in using a single verse from the Holy Scriptures, so is there also a danger in using a single saying of a saintly Father.

> And consider that the longsuffering of our Lord is salvation—as also our beloved brother Paul, according to the wisdom given to him, has written to you, as also in all his epistles, speaking in them of these things, in which are some things hard to understand, which untaught and unstable people twist to their own destruction, as they do also the rest of the Scriptures.[38]

8. The thought [i.e. writing] of the [Church] Father should be read in light of the issues of his time and the heresies he is facing; in light of its intellectual, linguistic, and philosophical context; and in light of the aim of his writings. For the writings of St. Cyril the Great, for example,

---

[37] J.A. McGuckin, *Saint Cyril of Alexandria and the Christological Controversy: its History, Theology, and Texts*. (Crestwood, NY: SVS Press: 2004) 352.

[38] 2 Peter 3:15–16.

before the appearance of the heresy of Nestorius, are completely different from [his writings] in the period of his facing this heresy up to his repose.

Theological terms, also, have their indication and meaning, which are sometimes different from one place to another, and from one [Church] Father to another. For until now, the Chalcedonians suppose that we believe in Eutyches' belief, merely because we use the expression one nature in our description of the nature of Christ which is the union of two natures, without mingling, without confusion, and without alteration.

"Whoever reads, let him understand."[39] "What is your reading of it?"[40]

9. Our Church does not believe in infallibility of men, even of the great, holy Fathers. The Holy Scriptures give us examples of fathers, prophets, and saints who sinned, and we ourselves sin daily. Blessed is the one who corrects themself, and does not insist on, and persist in, the error; therefore, we do not accept the opinion of a Father absolutely, unless there is unanimity in the Church on it.

> My brethren, let not many of you become teachers, knowing that we shall receive a stricter judgment. For we all stumble in many things. If anyone does not stumble

---

39 Matthew 24:15.
40 Luke 10:26.

The Sources of the Teaching of the Church

in word, he is a perfect man, able also to bridle the whole body. Indeed, we put bits in horses' mouths that they may obey us, and we turn their whole body.[41]

10. We believe in the continuing work of the Holy Spirit in the fathers of the Church. Therefore, we should not stop, and become set, at a particular generation, for the Holy Spirit is still giving the Church of the treasure of His goodness, that He may explain the same Divine truth, without change and without innovation, but in a manner fitting of the era, the issues, and the problems that face men.

> But the Helper, the Holy Spirit, whom the Father will send in My name, He will teach you all things, and bring to your remembrance all things that I said to you.[42]

> And I will pray the Father, and He will give you another Helper, that He may abide with you forever—the Spirit of truth, whom the world cannot receive, because it neither sees Him nor knows Him; but you know Him, for He dwells with you and will be in you.[43]

St. Cyril the Great says, "A man must interpret the Holy Scriptures though others have done so

---

41 James 3:1–3.
42 John 14:26.
43 John 14:16–17.

already."[44]

For the servants of this generation, of bishops, priests, deacons, and men and women servants, are called to declare the truth of the Scriptures and the teaching of the Fathers, in a manner fitting of the current time, with understandable expressions, and renewed meditations, without restraint or restriction.

For our early Fathers did not reiterate each other's words, but each [Church] Father had his own expression, language, and explanation which did not go outside the frame of sound teaching. Therefore, the contemporary teacher is not considered "patristic," by merely reciting the sayings of the Fathers, but rather he should digest their teachings and reformulate them in a suitable manner for the youth and the people of his generation.

11. We study the Fathers so that we may conform to their faith, their life, and their morals. Therefore, the one who studies [the works of] the Fathers must not speak with anger, sarcasm, or disdain, even toward those of contrary opinion.

> "Remember those who rule over you, who have spoken the word of God to you, whose faith follow, considering the outcome of

---

[44] Cyril of Alexandria, *Commentary of Isaiah*. In *Patrologia graeca* 71.12A, J.-P. Migne, ed. (Paris, 1857–1886) [Translated from Arabic text]. Cf. Cyril of Alexandria, *Commentary on Isaiah* 1, R.C. Hill, trans. (Brookline, MA: Holy Cross Orthodox Press, 2008), 17.

their conduct."[45]

St. Athanasius the Apostolic says:

But in addition to the study and true knowledge of the Scriptures, there is needed a good life and a pure soul and the virtue which is according to Christ, so that the mind, guided by it, may be able to attain and comprehend what it desires, as far as it is possible for human nature to learn about the God Word.[46]

3. The Liturgies

The liturgies of the Church are another reliable source and have the same value as the canons of the [Church] Councils, because they have earned the characteristic of unanimity, considering that all generations have prayed with the same words, expressing the same faith, in the spirit of godliness. Therefore, teaching what is contrary to that with which we pray in the official liturgies, is not permitted, especially the ancient texts which have Coptic and Greek roots, that is, with the exception of recent texts which were introduced in the eras when the Coptic language was weak.

---

45 Hebrews 13:7.
46 Saint Athanasius, *On the Incarnation,* J. Behr, trans. (Yonkers, NY: SVS Press, 2011), 110.

> "So continuing daily with one accord in the temple, and breaking bread from house to house, they ate their food with gladness and simplicity of heart."[47]

4. The Canons of the Local and Ecumenical Councils which are Affirmed by the Church

These canons reside above every teaching, because that which was discussed in a council and was determined, earns the characteristic of collectiveness. And often the canons entail excommunications of whoever teaches what is contrary to the decision of the council; while, without unanimity, there is no principle of excommunication of the one who teaches what is contrary to that of a [Church] Father.

> For it seemed good to the Holy Spirit, and to us, to lay upon you no greater burden than these necessary things.[48]

> But even if we, or an angel from heaven, preach any other gospel to you than what we have preached to you, let him be accursed [Gr. anathema].[49]

---

47 Acts 2:46.
48 Acts 15:28.
49 Galatians 1:8.

How are Decrees of Councils Formulated?

And generally, in Church Councils, the topics presented are examined in an exceedingly detailed manner and with theological research presented by esteemed Fathers. And no decision of the Council is made without meticulous examination; a decision does not depend on a single verse or one person's opinion.

Therefore, when a decree or a canon is passed by an ecumenical or local Church Council, the affair is final and cannot be re-examined.

In light of these references of the Church—the Holy Scriptures, the [Church] Fathers, the liturgies, and the canons of the Councils—we should submit and obey [them], and collect our opinions around one, simple understanding [brought about by them]. For our youth have enough [to deal with already], of what is in the world, of atheistic skepticism, attacks against the Holy Scriptures, skepticism about the divinity of the Lord Christ, in addition to the whirlpools of the attraction of obscenities and materialistic busyness.

So there is no reason for Church servants to clash [with each other] on principles of the faith that are firm in the Church. For the victims are the youth and the congregation, who become confused because of the discrepancy of thoughts and the exchange of accusations; and the only beneficiary in these conflicts is the current of atheism.

Therefore, let us return to the innocence of infancy and grasp our faith with the guilelessness of the child who has understanding and who is not [prone to] philosophizing.

> For it is written: "I will destroy the wisdom of the wise, and bring to nothing the understanding of the prudent." Where is the wise? Where is the scribe? Where is the disputer of this age? Has not God made foolish the wisdom of this world?[50]

> At that time Jesus answered and said, "I thank You, Father, Lord of heaven and earth, that You have hidden these things from the wise and prudent and have revealed them to babes."[51]

> And no one knows the Son except the Father. Nor does anyone know the Father except the Son, and the one to whom the Son wills to reveal Him.[52]

Grant, O Lord, that You fill us with Your grace, with knowledge, understanding, and spiritual wisdom, according to Your true promise.

---

[50] 1 Corinthians 1:19.
[51] Matthew 11:25.
[52] Matthew 11:27.

4

The Issue of the Sin of our Father Adam

Let us begin with our relationship with Adam's sin. Were we affected by his sin, or by its consequences only, that is, death and corruption, or were we not affected at all?

There are three groups:

The first group believes that we have no relationship at all with Adam's sin. This belief is usually widespread among non-Christians. It is also an extension of a heresy from the fourth and fifth centuries by a heretic named Pelagius, whom the Church excommunicated, along with his most famous disciple Celestius.

The second group believes that we have no relationship with Adam's sin, but we inherited from him the consequences of his sin, those being, death and corruption. Their explanation is that sin is an act, and we did not participate in the act because we were not in existence yet. We descended, however, from a mortal and corruptible root, so we inherited death and corruption.

The third group believes that we were in Adam when he was created, when he fell, when he died, and when he became corrupt; so we were accounted sinners, mortal, and corruptible, in him. Although we were not yet born as individuals descending from his seed, human nature, in its entirety, was in him. This understanding, according to the Church Fathers, is called the oneness of the human race. And this is what the Holy Scriptures, the explanations of the Fathers and the Orthodox liturgical texts, declare; and this is the understanding which our Coptic Orthodox Church believes, according to what we will see in this concise study.

Concerning the Issue of Our Relationship with Adam's Sin

I hope that we do not drift into "disputes rather than godly edification which is in faith."[53]

Life is too short for us to re-examine the issues that were settled upon in the holy Councils which our Church affirms. Time we should devote to prayer, praise, joy in Christ, works of care and

---

53 1 Timothy 1:4.

teaching which is according to godliness.

Summary of that which we believe, in this respect

1. We believe that we were in Adam when he was created, and when he sinned, died, and became corrupt; therefore, we are born of him sinful, dead, and corrupt. (The oneness of the human race).

2. The Son of God, the Word, came incarnate from the Virgin Mary, that He may be a new head for a new humankind.

3. Everyone who accepts the Son of God by faith, and unites with Him in Baptism, becomes, in Christ, a son of God the Father, with the condition that he continues to abide in Christ, through the Eucharist and continual repentance.

4. When we become sons of God in our Lord Jesus Christ, we receive in Him—that is, in Christ—righteousness, resurrection, and eternal life, as opposed to what we contracted in Adam: sin, death, and corruption.

5. By grace we become children of God and enjoy His good things in the Church, in the present time: the new nature, adoption by God the Father, membership in the body of Christ, and the promise of the inheritance of the kingdom of heaven in Christ.

6. And in the resurrection of the dead, at the last

day, we receive the grace of incorruptibility, and we are granted to sit with Him on His throne, and "we shall be like Him, for we shall see Him as He is."[54]

This faith we will prove by documentation from the sources of teaching in the Church, as we have already explained: The Holy Scriptures, the explanation of the Fathers with unanimity, the liturgies, and the canons of the ecumenical and local Councils which our Church affirms.

Let us begin with the Councils.

The Local Council of Carthage

Concerning the inheritance of Adam's sin, Pelagius and his disciple Celestius and their followers were condemned when they denied the inheritance of Adam's sin and proclaimed the heresy that children have no need of Baptism or that Baptism of children is not for the remission of sins.

The following was stated in the Second Council of Carthage in AD 418 (Canon 110):

> If any man says that new-born children need not be baptized, or that they should indeed be baptized for the remission of sins, but that they have in them no original sin inherited from Adam which must be washed away in the bath of regeneration, so that in their case the formula of baptism "for the remission

---

54 1 John 3:2.

of sins" must not be taken literally, but figuratively, let him be anathema; because, according to Rom. v. 12[55], the sin of Adam has passed upon all.[56]

Note: the text of the Epistle to the Romans here is according to the Latin translation, which is in agreement with the Coptic and ancient Greek translations. H.G. Bishop Gregorius, who has a Ph.D. in the Greek language, translates it thus: "And thus death spread to all men through whom all sinned in him." He explains this, saying, "This Holy Scripture affirms the principle of the spread of sin from the first man Adam to all men." He also comments, saying, "It is to be noted that in the [Arabic] Beirut translation [of the Bible][57] this verse is amputated... But the Greek and the Coptic texts, and the Latin translation known as Vulgate translation, all have the text in the way we have confirmed."[58] His Grace, then, included the texts in the three languages:

In Greek:

---

55 Romans 5:12.

56 C.J. Hefele, *A History of the Councils of the Church* 2, H.N. Oxenham, trans. (Edinburgh: T&T Clark, 1896), 458.

57 Also: Van Dyck version.

58 Bishop Gregorius, *Mawsouat Al-Lahout Al-Akeadi – Sirai Al-Tajasod Wa Al-Fidah Al-Joz' Althani* [Encyclopedia of Doctrinal Theology 7: The Mysteries of Incarnation and Redemption Part 2]. (Egypt: Maktabat *Al-Motana'ih Anba Gregorius* [The Library of the Late Abba Gregorius], 2004), 237. [Translated from Arabic text].

"καί οὕτως εἰς πάντας ἀνθρώπους ὁ θάνατος διῆλθεν ἐφ' ᾧ πάντες ἥμαρτον"

In Latin:

In quo omnes peccaverunt

In Coptic:

ⲀⲨ ⲡⲓⲙⲟⲩ ϣⲉ ⲉϧⲟⲩⲛ ⲉ ⲣⲱⲙⲓ ⲛⲓⲃⲉⲛ ⲫⲏⲉⲧⲁⲩⲣⲛⲟⲃⲓ ⲛ̀ϧⲏⲧϥ.

Therefore, there is no way here to claim that the word death was dropped from the Latin text, and that the Council of Carthage and St. Augustine were mistaken and confused, as those say who do not believe in the inheritance of Adam's sin.

This claim is unseemly and unacceptable. For of the simplest Christian principles is that we must not accuse a holy council of error, only because it has adopted an opinion contrary to ours.

Also there is no room for saying that the Council of Carthage expresses the thought of Western theology, because at that time (the fifth century) the Church was nothung but a one, only catholic [Church], East and West, and there was no difference except in geography and language. For the East wrote and spoke in the Greek language, while the West in the Latin language. And if differences were found in concepts and convictions between the East and the West because of the difference in culture, there was however concord and complementation of concepts. And they did not accuse each other of heresy, unless the opinion was heretical and was not approved by the Fathers of the East and West together.

It is worthy to note that the Great Schism between the East (Constantinople) and the West (Rome) took place in the beginning of the eleventh century, while the Council of Carthage and St. Augustine were in the fifth century.

The Ecumenical Council of Ephesus

Above all that, the Council of Ephesus, held in AD 431, headed by Pope Cyril the Pillar of Faith, agreed to the decrees of the Council of Carthage. In the Council's letter, which was sent by the Council of Ephesus to Celestine the First, Pope of Rome, the following was stated, informing him of what had taken place in the Council of Ephesus:

> Moreover, the minutes of the actions on the depositions of the unholy Pelagians and Celestians, Celestius, Pelagius, Julian, Presidius, Florus, Marcellinus, Orentius, and those who hold the same opinions with them, were read in the Holy Synod, and we also have deemed it right that those things which have been decreed against them by your God-reveringness shall remain strong

and firm. And we are all voters on the same side with you, and hold them deposed.[59]

It happened, in the first session of the Council of Ephesus, that the letter of St. Celestine Bishop of Rome to Nestorius, was read:

> Juvenal, Bishop of Jerusalem, said: Let the Letter of the most holy and most dear-to-God Archbishop of the Romans, Celestine, be read, which he has sent concerning the faith. Peter, a Presbyter of Alexandria, and Chief of the Secretaries, read [as follows]:
>
> A Translation of an Epistle of Celestine, Bishop of Rome, to Nestorius.
>
> Celestine to the beloved brother Nestorius: The Universal Faith had peace for some days of our lifetime, after the unholy and often condemned doctrine of Pelagius and Celestius, for both the East and the West, had smitten them with the followers of their opinions with the dart of a unanimous sentence. Straightway Atticus[60] of holy memory, the teacher of the Universal Faith, and verily successor of the Blessed John, in that same course of thinking and acting also, so pursued them on behalf of the Common

---

59 *The Third World Council* 2, J. Chrystal, trans. (Jersey City, NJ: James Chrystal, 1904), 177–182.

60 Bishop of Constantinople, who reposed in AD 425.

The Issue of the Sin of our Father Adam

King [God], that no permission was granted them to stay there [Constantinople].[61]

Also, in the eighth passage of this letter, [the following is written]:

> And furthermore, in relation to those heretics [that is, the Pelagians], regarding whom you, as not knowing [yourself] the matters concerning them, have wished to ask us, [we would say that] a righteous condemnation and decision has thrust them out from their own thrones, on the ground of their having spoken unrighteous things.... We have read how you believe well in regard to original sin, and how you show that our nature itself is whelmed [that is, perished] in debt, and that you rightly impute that debt to him who is descended from the race of the debtor [that is, Adam].[62]

St. Cyril the Great, also, said in the Council of Ephesus, in the fifth session:

> For we have never yet held the errors of Apolinarius, nor those of Arius, nor those of Eunomius, but from the time when we were little we have learned the sacred Scriptures,

---

61 *The Third World Council* 1, J. Chrystal, trans. (Jersey City, NJ: James Chrystal, 1895), 178–180.
62 *The Third World Council* 1, J. Chrystal, trans. (Jersey City, NJ: James Chrystal, 1895), 193.

and have been brought up in the hands of orthodox and holy fathers. And we anathemize Apolinarius, and Arius, and Eunomius, and Macedonius, Sabellius, Photinus, Paul, and the Manicheans, and every other heresy, and, besides them, Nestorius the contriver of the new blasphemies, and those who commune with him and agree with him, and those who hold the errors of Celestius, that is of Pelagius. We have never held the errors of those men. Nor have we now by a change of mind become willing to hold the right doctrines; but, as I have said, we have been brought up in the right and apostolic dogmas of the Church.[63]

His Grace Bishop Gregorius, General Bishop of Theological Studies, Coptic Culture, and Scientific Research, says:

When the first Council of Ephesus was held, which is the third Ecumenical Council, headed by Pope Cyril the First (AD 376–444), known as Cyril the Great, the Alexandrian, and the Pillar of the Faith, and that was in Ephesus in AD 431, the decision of the local Council of Carthage was read and affirmed, and its sentence on Pelagius, Celestius, and

---

[63] *The Third World Council* 2, J. Chrystal, trans. (Jersey City, NJ: James Chrystal, 1904), 155.

the followers of their heresy was affirmed. And it came in the acts of the first Council of Ephesus, the third Ecumenical [Council], that it approved the decision of the Council of Carthage unanimously.[64]

The scholar and Hegumen, **Fr. Tadros Yacoub Malaty** says:

On the other hand, Pelagius (AD 360–430) and his followers claimed that Adam's sin is personal, affecting him alone, without it coursing through the life of his children. Therefore, infants are born without original sin, so they do not need to be baptized, being like Adam before the fall. St. Augustine stood fighting this heresy, confirming from the Holy Scriptures that man is conceived in sin and that humankind is burdened with the ancestral sin (Romans 5:12). By this, like the mature [person], the infant needs the cross of our Lord Jesus Christ and the enjoyment of His resurrection through Baptism. Therefore, he says, "The baptized infants who die before reaching manhood escape the condemnation under

---

64 Bishop Gregorius, *Mawsouat Al-Lahout Al-Akeadi Al-Joz' Al-Thalith– Fi Asrar Al-Kanisa Al-Saba'a* [Encyclopedia of Doctrinal Theology 3: On the Seven Mysteries of the Church]. (Egypt: *Maktabat Al-Motana'ih Anba Gregorius* [The Library of the Late Abba Gregorius], 2005), 53–54. [Translated from Arabic text].

which humankind fell." And the Council of Carthage (AD 418–426) issued a canon that makes the Baptism of infants obligatory, to cleanse them of the ancestral sin. And the Council of Ephesus affirmed the decisions of the Council in AD 431.[65]

The scholar and Hegumen, **Fr. Tadros Yacoub Malaty** also says:

The Judgment: St. Augustine refuted the heresy of Pelagius. This heresy was condemned, with [that of] Celestius, in the Council of Carthage in AD 411, in the Council of Carthage in AD 416, [and] in the Council of Mileve in Numidia in AD 416; in AD 417, Innocent I, Pope of Rome, sentenced them with excommunication; [this heresy was also condemned] in the Council of Carthage in AD 418, by all its members of about 214 (and it was said 224); [it was condemned in] the letter of Pope Zosimus in AD 418; and it was definitively destroyed after it was condemned in the Council of Ephesus in AD 431.[66]

---

65 Fr. Tadros Malaty, *Al-Rouh Al-Kodos Bain Al-Milad Al-Jadid wa Al-Tajdid Al-Mostamir* [The Holy Spirit: Between the New Birth and Continual Renewal]. (Alexandria, Egypt: St. George Coptic Orthodox Church Sporting, 2003), 94. [Translated from Arabic text].

66 Fr. Tadros Malaty, *Naddra Shamila Li-Ilm Al-Patrology Fi Al-Sitat Al-Koron Al-Oula* [Panoramic View of Patristics in the First Six Centuries]. (Alexandria, Egypt: St. George Coptic Orthodox Church

And the Council of Ephesus also issued canons (first and fourth) to depose Celestius, the disciple of Pelagius, and all who agree with him and his teachings:

First Canon:

If any Metropolitan of a Province, forsaking the holy and Ecumenical Synod, has joined the assembly of the apostates, or shall join the same hereafter; or, if he has adopted, or shall hereafter adopt, the doctrines of Celestius, he has no power in any way to do anything in opposition to the bishops of the province, since he is already cast forth from all ecclesiastical communion and made incapable of exercising his ministry; but he shall himself be subject in all things to those very bishops of the province and to the neighboring orthodox metropolitans, and shall be degraded from his episcopal rank.[67]

Fourth Canon:

If any of the clergy should fall away, and publicly or privately presume to maintain the doctrines of Nestorius or Celestius, it is declared just by the holy Synod that these

---

Sporting, 2008), 348. [Translated from Arabic text].
67   *The Canons of the Two Hundred Holy and Blessed Fathers Who Met at Ephesus* 1 (NPNF[2] 14:225).

also should be deposed.[68,69]

---

68 *The Canons of the Two Hundred Holy and Blessed Fathers Who Met at Ephesus* 4 (NPNF[2] 14:229).

69 For further reading, see also:

✤ Hegumen Saleeb Souryal, *Dirasat fi Al-Kawanin Al-Kanasia fi Asr Al-Majamih Al-Kanasia Al-Kitab Al-Thalith* [Studies in the Canons of the Church in the Era of the Councils of the Church Vol. 3]. (Egypt: Clerical and Theological College of the Coptic Orthodox, 1992), 126.

✤ "In addition, this Council confirmed the condemnation of Pelagius and of Celestius, which they had received from many local synods and regional councils, and especially from the Council held in Carthage." [Nicodemus the Hagiorite and Agapius he Monk, *The Rudder (Pedalion) of the Metaphorical Ship of the One Hot Catholic and Apostolic Church of the Orthodox Christians, or All the Sacred and Divine Canons*, D. Cummings, trans. (Chicago, IL: Orthodox Christian educational Society, 1957), 226].

✤ "The Western Acts on the condemnation of the Pelagians and Celestians, of Pelagius, Caelestius, and his adherents, Julianus, Persidius, Florus, Marcellinus, and Orentius, etc., were read, and the papal judgment on them universally approved." [C.J. Hefele, *A History of the Councils of the Church* 3. (Edinburgh: T&T Clark, 1883), 69].

✤ "After the records of the negotiations were read in the holy synod respecting the deposition (χαθαίρεσει) of the unholy Pelagians and Caelestians, Caelestius, Pelagius, Julian, Persidius, Marcellinus, Orontius, and those of the like sentiments, we also believed, that what has been decided by your holiness respecting them, must remain in force, and we all agree with you in declaring them deposed (χαθηρημένους)." [G.F. Wiggers, *An Historical Presentation of Augustinism and Pelagianism from the Original Sources*, R. Emerson, trans. (New York, NY: Gould, Newman, and Saxton, 1840), 266–267].

What Does the Sentence of Excommunication Against a Person Mean?

And needless to say, excommunicating someone by a council's decision means banning his teaching and not merely his person, because there are no personal enmities with people. Therefore, excommunicating Arius, for example, means the excommunication of the Arian thought and all who follow it. So, there is no room here to claim that the Council of Ephesus agreed to excommunicate people only, without agreeing with the decrees of the Council of Carthage concerning the teaching, as is taught by those who reject the inheritance of Adam's sin. Also, there is no council's decree or a saying of the Fathers, throughout the history of the Church, that excommunicates anyone who teaches about the inheritance of Adam's sin, while the opposite is true in the local Council of Carthage, which was approved by the ecumenical Council of Ephesus.

> "But even if we, or an angel from heaven, preach any other gospel to you than what we have preached to you, let him be accursed. As we have said before, so now I say again, if anyone preaches any other gospel to you than what you have received, let him be accursed [Gr. ἀνάθεμα]."[70]

This is what was determined in the Councils of

---

70 Galatians 1:8–9.

Carthage and Ephesus concerning our relationship with Adam's sin. As for the rest of the sources of the teaching of the Church (the Holy Scriptures, the teachings of the Fathers, and the liturgies), I would like to state them under three main headings: In Adam we were created; in Adam we sinned, died, and were corrupted; in Christ we are justified, we are raised, and we will live for eternity.

In Adam we were Created

We were in Adam when he was created; therefore, we became created in him. (Oneness of the human race).

> Worthy of note is that St. Athanasius, instead of using 'Adam,' uses 'humans,' in most of his writings, especially in *On the Incarnation*, which is an expression that indicates not a single human, but all humans, thereby he confirms the oneness of the human race.[71]

St. Athanasius the Apostolic says:

> Thus too has the race made after God's image come to be, namely men; for though Adam only was formed out of earth, yet in him was

---

71 Athanasius the Apostolic, *Tagasod Al-Kalima* [The Incarnation of the Word], J.M. Faltas, trans. (Cairo, Egypt: St. Anthony Press–The Orthodox Center for Patristic Studies in Cairo, 2003), 10. [This footnote by Dr. Flatas, the translator of *The Incarnation of the Word* into Arabic, was retrieved and translated from Arabic].

involved the succession of the whole race.[72]

St. Cyril the Great says, "Soar in your mind then to the first Adam, and see in him the entire humankind."[73]

And this is exactly what we pray with in the Coptic [Divine] Liturgy:

"Who formed us, created us, and placed us in the Paradise of joy."[74]

> You, as a Lover of Mankind, have created me, as man.... Because of the multitude of Your tender mercies, You have brought me into existence when I was not.[75]

> You have raised heaven as a roof for me, and established the earth for me to walk upon. For my sake, You have bound the sea. For my sake, You have manifested the nature of animals. You have subjected all things under my feet.... You are He who formed me, and laid Your hand upon me, and inscribed in me the image of Your authority. You have

---

72 Athanasius *Four Discourses Against the Arians* 2.19.48 (NPNF[2] 4:374–375).

73 Cyril the Great, *Al-Sojoud Wa Al-Ibada Bi-Al Rouh Wa Al-Hak* [Worshipping and Serving in Spirit and in Truth], Ibrahim G.A., trans. (Cairo, Egypt: St. Anthony Press–The Orthodox Center for Patristic Studies, 2017), 93. [Translated from Arabic text].

74 The Divine Liturgy According to St. Basil – Agios (Holy).

75 The Divine Liturgy According to St. Gregory – Agios (Holy).

placed in me the gift of speech, and opened for me Paradise to enjoy.[76]

Note that the priest, here, speaks with the tongue of all of humankind in the person of Adam.

In Adam we Sinned

And as we were in Adam when he was created, so we were created in him; likewise we were in him when he sinned, died, and became corrupted, so we sinned in him, died, and became corrupted.

St. Cyril the Great says:

> For so did He [Christ] as one of us set Himself as an avenger in our stead, against that murderous and rebellious serpent, who had brought sin upon us, and thereby had caused corruption and death to reign over the dwellers upon earth, that we by His means, and in Him, might gain the victory, whereas of old we were vanquished, and fallen in Adam.[77]

St. Cyril the Great also says, "By eating we were conquered in Adam, by abstinence we conquered in Christ."[78]

---

76 Ibid.
77 Cyril of Alexandria, *A Commentary upon the Gospel According to S. Luke* 1, R.P. Smith, trans. (Oxford, ENG: Oxford Press, 1859), 49.
78 Ibid., 54.

[He also says:]

We became partakers of Adam's offense, and because of his sins we were punished, the curse reaching all, and wrath extending over his seed. Therefore, the Only-begotten descended and placed Himself in submission to God the Father, and became man and dwelt among us. For it says, "[He] became obedient to the point of death,"[79] blotting out the consequences of the disobedience of all[80], and the disobedience of each one separately[81], and by this He saved us. Paul testifies about this, saying, "Therefore, as through one man's offense judgement came to all men, resulting in condemnation, even so through one Man's righteous act the free gift came to all men, resulting in justification of life. For as by one man's disobedience many were made sinners, so also by one Man's obedience many will be made righteous."[82,83]

---

79 Philippians 2:8.

80 By "the disobedience of all" is meant the disobedience of all in Adam.

81 By "the disobedience of each one separately" is meant our actually-committed sins, of each one separately.

82 Romans 5:18–19.

83 Cyril the Great, *Al-Sojoud Wa Al-Ibada Bi-Al Rouh Wa Al-Hak* [Worshipping and Serving in Spirit and in Truth], G.A. Ibrahim, trans. (Egypt: The Orthodox Center for Patristic Studies, 2017), 461. [Translated from text].

[And he also says:]

For that we sinned in Adam first, and trampled underfoot the Divine commandment. For He was dishonored for our sake, in that He took our sins upon Him, as the prophet says[84], and was afflicted on our account. For as He wrought out our deliverance from death, giving up His own Body to death, so likewise, I think, the blow with which Christ was smitten, in fulfilling the dishonor that He bore, carried with it our deliverance from the dishonor by which we were burdened through the transgression and original sin of our forefather. For He, being One, was yet a perfect Ransom for all men, and bore our dishonor.[85]

And he says, "For the whole nature of man became guilty in the person of him who was first formed [Adam]."[86]

St. Augustine says:

"For all have sinned"—whether in Adam or in themselves—"and come short of the glory of God."[87] The entire mass, therefore, incurs penalty and if the deserved punishment of condemnation were rendered to all, it would

---

[84] Isaiah 53:4 LXX.

[85] Cyril of Alexandria, *Commentary on the Gospel according to S. John* 2. (London, ENG: Walter Smith, 1885), 585.

[86] Cyril of Alexandria, *A Commentary upon the Gospel According to S. Luke* 1, R.P. Smith, trans. (Oxford, ENG: Oxford Press, 1859), 171.

[87] Romans 3:23.

without doubt be righteously rendered. They, therefore, who are delivered therefrom by grace are called, not vessels of their own merits, but "vessels of mercy."[88,89]

St. Gregory Nazianzus says:

We were all without exception created anew, who partake of the same Adam, and were led astray by the serpent and slain by sin, and are saved by the heavenly Adam and brought back by the tree of shame[90] to the tree of life from whence we had fallen.[91]

St. Irenaeus (of the second century AD) says:

Inasmuch as it was by these things that we disobeyed God, and did not give credit to His word, so was it also by these same that He brought in obedience and consent as respects His Word; by which things He clearly shows forth God Himself, whom indeed we had offended in the first Adam, when he did not perform His commandment. In the second Adam, however, we are reconciled, being made obedient even unto death. For we were

---

88 Romans 9:23.

89 Augustine, *A Treatise on Nature and Grace* 4–5 (NPNF[1] 5:122–123).

90 I.e. the cross.

91 Gregory Nazianzen *Oration XXXIII. Against The Arians, and Concerning Himself* 9 (NPNF[2] 7:331).

debtors to none other but to Him whose commandment we had transgressed at the beginning.[92]

St. Ambrose says:

In Adam I fell, in Adam I was cast out of Paradise, in Adam I died; how shall the Lord call me back, except He find me in Adam; guilty as I was in him, so now justified in Christ.[93]

St. Jacob Bishop of Serug says:

David knew by the inspiration of his Lord that the Levitical sacrifices do not liberate the world which needs salvation, and that the sin, which was introduced by the serpent, and which is inherited from generation to generation, cannot be remitted through ordinary Levitical sacrifices; there must be redemption for it, and the redemption must be for every individual. And he ascertained that the Son will Himself be the Redeemer, to become a High Priest; therefore, he likened Him to Melchizedek in the richness of beauties.[94]

---

92 Irenaeus *Against Heresies*. In *Ante-Nicene Fathers* 1, P. Schaff, ed. (Peabody, MA: Hendrickson Publishers, 2012), 544.

93 Ambrose *On the Belief in the Resurrection* 6 (NPNF[2] 10:175).

94 Jacob of Serug, *Mokhtarat Min Kasa'id Mar Yakob Oskof Sirouj* [A Selection of the Poems of Mar Jacob Bishop of Serug], Metropolitan

Mar Seveus Moses Bin Kiffa, the philosopher and scholar, metropolitan of Mosul and Barman, of the ninth century AD, says:

> What is the fasting which we fast, what is its reason, whence we began fasting, and why do we fast? We say, for many considerations: First, [it is] because by eating, **we trespassed the commandment and sinned**, and by fasting, we keep the commandment and are justified. For fasting and eating are at odds [with each other]; likewise trespassing the commandment and keeping it, [and] justification and sin. Thus, by eating **we sinned**, so we fast that we may be justified.[95]

St. Athanasius the Apostolic says:

> He now offered the sacrifice on behalf of all, delivering his own temple to death in the stead of all, in order to make all not liable to and free from the ancient transgression.[96]

Malatios Barnaba, trans. (Aleppo, Syria: *Dar El-Raha*,1993), 81. [Translated from Arabic text].

95 *Al-Mawa'id Lil-Failasouf Al-Alama Mar Sawaius Moussa Bin Kiffa Motram Al-Mosul wa Barman* [The Sermons of the Philosopher and Scholar Mar Severus Moses Bin Kiffa, Metropolitan of Mosul and Barman], Behnam Daniel of Bartela, translator into Arabic. (Duhok, Iraq: Oriental Cultural Center, 2013), 148. [Translated from Arabic text]. The scholar Mar Severus mentions other considerations, as reasons for fasting, but we have included the first consideration only, as it serves our case.

96 Saint Athanasius, *On the Incarnation*, Behr J., trans. (Yonkers,

St. Athanasius also says:

The God of all then,—creating us by His own Word, and knowing our destinies better than we, and foreseeing that, being made "good," we should in the event be transgressors of the commandment, and be thrust out of paradise for dis- obedience,— being loving and kind, prepared beforehand in His own Word, by whom also He created us, the Economy of our salvation; that though by the serpent's deceit we fell from Him, we might not remain quite dead, but having in the Word the redemption and salvation which was afore prepared for us.[97]

The expressions of the esteemed Fathers here are clear and explicit, not liable to ambiguity, and do not [themselves] need explanation apart from what they wrote.

The Holy Scriptures refer to us as being weak,[98] ungodly, sinners, enemies, and not only as dead and corrupt. That is, the problem of man originally is sin, and not death and corruption only, as those teach who do not believe in the inheritance of sin.

"For when we were still without strength, in due

NY: SVS Press, 2011), 70.

97 Athanasius *Four Discourses Against the Arians* 2.22.75 (NPNF[2] 4: 389).

98 Or: without strength.

The Issue of the Sin of our Father Adam

time Christ died for the ungodly."[99]

"But God demonstrates His own love toward us, in that while we were still sinners, Christ died for us."[100]

"For if when we were enemies we were reconciled to God through the death of His Son, much more, having been reconciled, we shall be saved by His life."[101]

The salvific work of the Lord Christ can be described as having "put away[102] sin," and not only as putting away death and corruption.

"He then would have had to suffer often since the foundation of the world; but now, once at the end of the ages, He has appeared to put away sin by the sacrifice of Himself."[103]

"So Christ was offered once to bear the sins of many. To those who eagerly wait for Him He will appear a second time, apart from sin, for salvation."[104]

And the [Divine] Liturgy of our Church testifies to the same faith: the oneness of the human race in Adam and that we sinned in him.

---

99   Romans 5:6.
100 Romans 5:8.
101 Romans 5:10.
102 Or: annulled.
103 Hebrews 9:26.
104 Hebrews 9:28.

When we disobeyed Your commandment by the deceit of the serpent, we fell from eternal life and were exiled from the Paradise of joy.[105]

[You] opened for me Paradise to enjoy ... You have manifested to me the tree of life, and made known to me the sting of death. Of one plant have You forbidden me to eat, that of which You have said to me, "Of it only do not eat." But according to my will, I did eat. I put Your law behind me by my own counsel, and became slothful toward Your commandments. I plucked for myself the sentence of death.... You have shown me the rising up from my fall.... You have abolished sin in the flesh.[106]

It is well-known that we pray with what we believe in. And there are no expressions in Coptic liturgies that may be described as only devotional, and not expressing the faith.

In Adam and not with him

Our Church does not teach that we partook as individuals in the act of Adam's sin, but we became sinners in him, and not with him, because we did not

---

[105] The Divine Liturgy According to St. Basil – Agios (Holy).
[106] The Divine Liturgy According to St. Gregory – Agios (Holy).

exist as individuals when he sinned and disobeyed the commandment. And of the Fathers who taught that we did not partake of Adam's sin, they mean [by this] the same as what the Church now teaches, that we did not partake with him in the eating, because we did not exist yet as individuals descending from his seed, but we were in him and the entire human nature sinned in him.

The Likeness of Sinful Flesh

If Adam's sin were not in us, why would it be said concerning the Lord Christ that He resembled us in everything, except for sin alone?

"For we do not have a High Priest who cannot sympathize with our weaknesses, but was in all points tempted as we are, yet without sin."[107]

"And you know that He was manifested to take away our sins, and in Him there is no sin."[108]

Some may think that the expression "He resembled us in everything, except for sin alone" means [only] that the Lord Christ did not commit actual sins, and does not mean that we inherited Adam's sin and the Lord Jesus did not share with us in this inheritance. He—glory be to Him—truly did not commit actual sins, but also He did not inherit Adam's sin, while we did inherit it; therefore, it was

---

107 Hebrews 4:15.
108 1 John 3:5.

said of Him that He took "the likeness of sinful flesh."

> For what the law could not do in that it was weak through the flesh, God did by sending His own Son in the likeness of sinful flesh, on account of sin: He condemned sin in the flesh.[109]

Our flesh is sinful flesh, and not only the flesh of death and corruption, and the Lord Jesus took our flesh without sin; therefore, it is said that He came in the likeness of sinful flesh.

St. John Chrysostom says in his explanation of the expression "the likeness of sinful flesh":

> But if he does say that it was "in the likeness" of flesh that he sent the Son, do not therefore suppose that His flesh was of a different kind. For as he called it "sinful," this was why he put the word "likeness." For sinful flesh it was not that Christ had, but like to our sinful flesh, yet sinless, and in nature the same with us.[110]

St. Athanasius the Apostolic says:

> But He who existed before the ages, God the Word, was seen as man from Nazareth

---

[109] Romans 8:3.

[110] John Chrysostom *Homilies on the Epistle of St. Paul the Apostle to the Romans* 13 (NPNF¹ 11:432).

having been born of Mary the Virgin, and the Holy Spirit, in Bethlehem of Judaea, from the seed of David and Abraham, and of Adam, as it is written: having taken from the Virgin all that God originally fashioned and made in order to the constitution of man, yet without sin: as also the Apostle says, In all points like to us, yet without sin.[111]

He also said:

He had been seen in the form of him that was condemned, but in that form as uncondemned and sinless; that the reconciliation of God to man might come to pass, and the freedom of the whole of man might be effected by means of man, in the newness of the image of His Son Jesus Christ our Lord.[112]

Origen says:

What he has said, "in the likeness of the flesh of sin,"[113] shows that we indeed have flesh of sin, but the Son of God had "the likeness of flesh of sin," not the flesh of sin. For all of us human beings who have been

---

111   Saint Athanasius, *Later Treatises of S. Athanasius, Archbishop of Alexandria*, Rev. Bright, trans. (Oxford, ENG: James Parker and Co., 1881), 122.

112   Ibid., 104–105.

113   Romans 8:3.

conceived from the seed of a man coming together with a woman, must of necessity employ that utterance which David says, "in iniquity I have been conceived and in sins did my mother conceive me."[114] He, however, who came to an immaculate body with no contact from a man, but only by the Holy Spirit coming upon the virgin and by the power of the Most High overshadowing, did indeed possess the nature of our body, but he possessed in no respect whatsoever the contamination of sin, which is passed down to those who are conceived by the operation of lust. For this reason, it is said that the Son of God came "in the likeness of flesh of sin."[115]

Origen also says:

But if instead the Apostle should be understood as having called our body the body of sin, it will assuredly be taken in agreement with the understanding which David speaks of in reference to himself, "For I was conceived in iniquities and in sins did my mother conceive me."[116] And the Apostle

---

114 Psalm 51:5 LXX.
115 Origen, *Commentary on the Epistle to the Romans, Book 6–10*, T.P. Halton, ed.; T. P. Scheck, trans. (Washington, D.C.: The Catholic University of America Press, 2002), 49.
116 Psalms 51:5.

himself says elsewhere, "Who will rescue me from the body of this death?"[117] and again he calls our body "the body of lowliness."[118] Moreover, he says of the Savior in a certain passage that he came "in the likeness of the flesh of sin, so that with respect to sin he might condemn sin in the flesh."[119] He is showing by this that our flesh is indeed a flesh of sin, but Christ's flesh is similar to the flesh of sin. For he was not conceived from the seed of a man, but the Holy Spirit came upon Mary and the power of the Most High overshadowed her so that what was born from her should be called the Son of the Most High.[120] In this way, then, Paul, through the inexpressible wisdom of God which was given to him, and looking at something secret, who knows what, calls our body "the body of sin" and "the body of death" and "the body of lowliness."[121]

Then **Origen** continues his explanation, saying: After all, even in the law it is commanded

---

117 Romans 7:24.

118 Philippians 3:21.

119 Romans 8:3.

120 Cf. Luke 1:35.

121 Origen, *Commentary on the Epistle to the Romans, Book 1–5*, T.P. Halton, ed.; T.P. Scheck, trans. (Washington, D.C.: The Catholic University of America Press, 2001), 365–366.

that sacrifices be offered for the child who was born: a pair of turtledoves or two young doves; one of which was offered for sin and the other as a burnt offering[122]. For which sin is this one dove offered? Was a newly born child able to sin? And yet it has a sin for which sacrifices are commanded to be offered, and from which it is denied that anyone is pure, even if his life should be one day long[123]. It has to be believed, therefore, that concerning this David also said what we recorded above, "in sins my mother conceived me." For according to the historical narrative no sin of his mother is declared. It is on this account as well that the Church has received the tradition from the apostles to give baptism even to little children. For they to whom the secrets of the divine mysteries were committed[124] were aware that in everyone was sin's innate defilement, which needed to be washed away through water and the Spirit[125]. Because of this defilement as well, the body itself is called the body of sin.[126]

---

122 See Leviticus 12:8.

123 See Job 14:4–5 LXX.

124 See 1 Corinthians 4:1.

125 See John 3:5.

126 Origen, *Commentary on the Epistle to the Romans, Book 1–5*, T.P. Halton, ed.; T.P. Scheck, trans. (Washington, D.C.: The Catholic University of America Press, 2001), 366–367.

The Issue of the Sin of our Father Adam

St. Philoxenus, Bishop of Mabbug (fifth century AD), says:

> Likewise also the Apostle himself writes to us in another place: "God sent His own Son in the likeness of sinful flesh, on account of sin, to condemn sin in the flesh." He sent the Son, God the Word, in the likeness of sinful flesh, and when He took the sinful flesh and made it His own, He wore it then, and in the flesh of His hypostasis, through the suffering and death, He annulled sin. He was not wearing a sinful flesh—God forbid! But He, in the incarnation of His hypostasis, made His own a pure and holy body [taken] from the sinful nature of the creatures. And through the life of His Nature and its righteousness, He baptized[127] His flesh. And when He made it His own, in the union of the one hypostasis, He returned and condemned, through His flesh, sin which used to reign over the flesh of humankind.[128]

St. Cyril the Great says:

> Since on account of the transgression in Adam, sin has reigned against all, and then the Holy Ghost fled away from the human

---

127 Arabic: *sabagha*.

128 Philoxenus, *Al-Rasa'il Al-Akidia Al-Josh Al-Awal* [The Doctrinal Letters, Vol. 1], Monk Rojeah Joseph, trans. (Darhon, Lebanon: Rohana Al-Shimali, 2007), 313. [Translated from Arabic text].

nature and it came therefore to be in all ill, and it needed that by the Mercy of God, it mounting up to its pristine condition should be accounted worthy of the Spirit:—the Only-Begotten Word of God became Man, and appeared to them on earth with Body of earth, and was made free from sin.[129]

When the Lord Jesus said, "And as Moses lifted up the serpent in the wilderness, even so must the Son of Man be lifted up, that whoever believes in Him should not perish but have eternal life,"[130] He meant that as the bronze serpent is like the deadly serpent in everything except that it does not have the venom of death in it, so is the flesh of the Lord like our flesh in everything except the venom of sin.

St. Macarius the Great says:

As no serpent of brass was ever commanded by the Lord to be made in the world until Moses, so a new and sinless body was never seen in the world until the [incarnation of the] Lord.[131]

---

129 Cyril of Alexandria, *Five Tomes Against Nestorius; Scholia on the Incarnation; Christ Is One; Fragments Against Diodore of Tarsus, Theodore of Mopsuestia, the Synousiasts.* (Oxford, ENG: James Parker and Co., 1881), 186.

130 John 3:14–15.

131 *Fifty Spiritual Homilies of St. Macarius the Egyptian*, A.J. Mason, trans. (London, ENG: Society for Promoting Christian Knowledge, 1921), 84.

St. Jacob, Bishop of Serug, says:

He portrayed His body as a brass serpent which he made, and through it was healed everyone who was bitten by serpents. The venom of serpents was not present in that serpent; neither was sin [present] in the body of our Lord who became like us.[132]

St. Gregory of Nyssa says:

The Law prefigures for us what is clear in the wood. This figure is a likeness of a serpent and not a serpent itself, as the great Paul himself says, "in the likeness of sinful flesh." Sin is the real serpent, and whoever deserts to sin takes on the nature of the serpent. Man, then, is freed from sin through him who assumed the form of sin.[133]

St. Macarius the Great also says:

How should we be anything but serpents, we who are not found in obedience to God, but in the disobedience which came by the serpent? How to bewail the calamity as it

---

[132] Mar Jacob of Serug, *Tarjamah min Al-Soriania ila Al-Arabia wa Dirasa ala Miamer Al-Milfan Mar Yakoub Al-Sorouji, Al-Jos'h Al-Awal* [A Translation from Syriac to Arabic and a Study on the Homilies of the Doctor (of the Church) Mar Jacob of Serug, Vol. 1], Fr. Soni B., trans. (Bagdad, Iraq: 2003), 1333. [Translated fro Arabic text].

[133] Gregory of Nyssa, *The Life of Moses*, R.J. Payne, ed.; A.J. Malherbe and E. Ferguson, trans. (Mahwah, NJ: Paulist Press, 1978), 124.

deserves, I cannot find. How to cry aloud and weep to Him that is able to expel the error lodged within me, I do not know.[134]

St. Cyril the Great says:

Paul says about the Son of God, "who, being in the form of God, did not consider it robbery to be equal with God, but made Himself of no reputation, taking the form of a bondservant, and coming in the likeness of men."[135] Then the Word of God became man. He did not come and dwell in a man, like that which happened with the prophets, but became truly that which we are, except for sin only.[136]

Some ask, [saying], "Are we punished for something we did not do?" The one asking this question, to begin with, believes in the inheritance of death and corruption. Why do we accept that we died and were corrupted in Adam without asking [questions] nor objecting, [but] then we ask, "Why were we made sinners in Adam?"

---

134 *Fifty Spiritual Homilies of St. Macarius the Egyptian*, A.J. Mason, trans. (London, ENG: Society for Promoting Christian Knowledge, 1921), 181.

135 Philippians 2:6–7.

136 St. Cyril the Alexandrian, *Al-Konouz fi Al-Thalooth* [The Treasures in the Trinity], J.A. Ibrahim, trans. (Cairo, Egypt: St. Anthony Press–The Orthodox Center for Patristic Studies in Cairo, 2011), 365. [Translated from Arabic text].

It is the same principle. Just as we were born in the state of death and corruption, we likewise were born sinners and disobedient. And the Holy Scripture teaches the same understanding; for in the epistle to the Romans, the Holy Spirit says, "Therefore, just as through one man sin entered the world, and death through sin, and thus death spread to all men, because all sinned."[137]

Note that he said that sin entered the world, that is, men, and did not say that death and corruption entered [the world]. Rather, death and corruption were subsequent to the entrance of sin—and death through sin.

St. Athanasius the Apostolic says:

For as by one man, as says Paul (and it is the truth), sin passed upon all men, so by the resurrection of our Lord Jesus Christ, we shall all rise. "For," he says, "this corruptible must put on incorruption, and this mortal must put on immortality."[138,139]

St. Gregory the Wonderworker says:

Wherefore, when it is said that He was "troubled in spirit,"[140] that "He was

---

137 Romans 5:12.
138 1 Corinthians 15:53.
139 Athanasius *Letters of Athanasius* 11.14 (NPNF² 4:538).
140 See John 11:33; 12:27; 13:21.

sorrowful in soul,"[141] that "He was wounded in body,"[142] He places before us designations of susceptibilities proper to our constitution, in order to show that He was made man in the world, and had His conversation with men,[143] yet without sin.[144]

St. Gregory the Wonderworker continues, saying:

> As sin entered into the world by flesh, and death came to reign by sin over all men, the sin in the flesh might also be condemned through the selfsame flesh in the likeness thereof;[145] and that that overseer of sin, the tempter, might be overcome, and death be cast down from its sovereignty, and the corruption in the burying of the body be done away, and the first-fruits of the resurrection be shown, and the principle of righteousness begin its course in the world through faith, and the kingdom of heaven be preached to men, and fellowship be established between God and men.[146]

---

141 See Matthew 26:38.

142 See Isaiah 53:5.

143 See Baruch 3:38.

144 *The writings of Gregory Thaumaturgus, Dionysius of Alexandria, and Archelaus*. In *Ante-Nicene Christian Library* 20. A. Roberts and J. Donaldson, eds. (Edinburgh: T. & T. Clark, 1871), 109.

145 See Romans 5:12; 8:3.

146 *The writings of Gregory Thaumaturgus, Dionysius of Alexandria,*

And in his interpretation of the testimony of St. John the Baptist concerning our Lord Jesus Christ—"Behold! The lamb of God who takes away the sin of the world!"[147]—**St. Augustine** says:

> Therefore, "Behold, the Lamb of God." He is not a scion[148] stemming from Adam; he took only the flesh from Adam, he did not assume his sin. He who has not assumed the sin from our clayey mass is the one who takes away our sin.[149]

St. John Chrysostom explains the following passage from Scripture, "For until the law sin was in the world, but sin is not imputed when there is no law. Nevertheless death reigned from Adam to Moses, even over those who had not sinned according to the likeness of the transgression of Adam, who is a type of Him who was to come."[150] And he says, "It is clear, that it was not this sin, the transgression, that is, of the Law, but that of Adam's disobedience, which marred all things. Now what is the proof of this? The fact that even before the Law all died."[151]

---

and Archelaus. In *Ante-Nicene Christian Library* 20. A. Roberts and J. Donaldson, eds. (Edinburgh: T. & T. Clark, 1871), 109.

147 John 1:29.

148 That is, an heir.

149 Augustine of Hippo, *Tractates on the Gospel of John 1–10*, J. W. Rettig, trans. (Washington, DC: The Catholic University of America Press, 1988), 101.

150 Romans 5:13–14

151 John Chrysostom *Homilies on the Epistle of St. Paul the Apostle to*

Our teacher Paul the Apostle continues, saying:

> Therefore, as through one man's offense judgment came to all men, resulting in condemnation, even so through one Man's righteous act the free gift came to all men, resulting in justification of life. For as by one man's disobedience many were made sinners, so also by one Man's obedience many will be made righteous.[152]

And here he also says that by the disobedience of the one, that is, Adam, many were made sinners, and not only dead and corrupted. And there is no opportunity here to interpret [the phrase] "many were made sinners" to mean their own sins only resulting from their being born in the state of death and corruption, because the comparison which our teacher Paul the Apostle here makes is between Adam's sin and Christ's righteousness, and not [between] our own sins and Christ's righteousness.

St. John Chrysostom tightly binds sin and death such that one cannot be mentioned without mentioning the other, when he says, "What then does the word 'sinners'[153] mean here? To me it seems to mean liable to punishment and condemned to death."[154]

---

the Romans 10 (NPNF¹ 11:402).
152 Romans 5:18–19.
153 St. John Chrysostom explains Romans 5:19.
154 John Chrysostom *Homilies on the Epistle of St. Paul the Apostle to*

The Issue of the Sin of our Father Adam

What about infants? Why do we baptize them?

"Behold, I was brought forth in iniquity, and in sin my mother conceived me."[155]

St. Augustine says:

Was David born of adultery; being born of Jesse[156], a righteous man, and his own wife? What is it that he says himself to have been in iniquity conceived, except that iniquity is drawn from Adam?... If infants are every way innocent, why do mothers run with them when sick to the Church? What by that Baptism, what by that remission is put away?... What does Baptism wash off? what does that Grace loose? There is loosed the offspring of sin. For if that infant could speak to you, it would say, and if it had the understanding which David had, it would answer you, Why pay attention to me, an infant? You indeed do not see my actions: but I in iniquity have been conceived, "And in sins has my mother nourished me in the womb."[157]

He also says:

---

the Romans 10 (NPNF[1] 11:403).

155 Psalms 51:5.

156 1 Samuel 16:18.

157 Augustine *Exposition on the Book of Psalms* 51.10 (NPNF[1] 8:192–193).

No one is pure in the sight of God, not even a babe of one day on earth; although these are counted as exceptions, and beyond the limits of our human measurements to enquire about the rank they are worthy of in the portion of the saints, promised in the future![158]

On this **St. Basil the Great** says:

"No one born of woman is without sin, even if his life is one day on earth;"[159] and David groans, saying: "I was brought forth in iniquity, and in sin my mother conceived me;" and as proclaimed by the apostle: "For all have sinned and fall short of the glory of God; being justified freely by His grace through the redemption that is in Christ Jesus, whom God set forth to be a propitiation by His blood."[160] Hence, the forgiveness of sins is given to those who believe; according to the words of the Lord Himself: "This is My blood of the new covenant, which is shed for many for the remission of sins."[161,162]

---

158 Fr. Tadros Malaty, *On the Book of Psalms*. (Alexandria, Egypt: St. George Coptic Orthodox Church–Sporting, 1991), 849.

159 Job 14:4.

160 Romans 3: 23–25.

161 Matthew 26:28.

162 Fr. Tadros Malaty, *On the Book of Psalms*. (Alexandria, Egypt:

The scholar Origen says:

Everyone who enters this world is said to be made with a certain contamination. This is also why Scripture says, "No one is clean from filth even if his life were only one day."[163] Therefore, from the fact that he is placed "in the womb of his mother"[164] and that he takes the material of the body from the origin of the paternal seed, he can himself be called "contaminated in his father and mother."[165] Or do you not know that when a male child is forty days old, he is offered at the altar that he may be purified[166] there as if he were polluted in this conception either by the paternal seed or the uterus of the mother? Therefore, every man "was polluted in his father and mother," but only Jesus my Lord came pure into the world in this birth and "was not polluted in his mother." For he entered "an uncontaminated body."[167] For he was the one who spoke long ago through Solomon, "But since I was better, I came into an undefiled body."[168,169]

1991), 849.
163 Cf. Job 14:4–5 LXX.
164 Cf. Job 3:11.
165 Cf. Leviticus 21:11.
166 Cf. Leviticus 12:2f.
167 For the Holy Spirit came upon her and sanctified her.
168 Wisdom 8:20.
169 Origen, *Homilies of Leviticus 1–16*, G.W. Barkley, trans.

St. Cyril the Great says:

Our nature suffered defilement through another way, [defilement] having reigned over all who were born [as] a fruit of the love of carnal pleasure [that is, a relation between a man and woman]. And this is exactly what shows of what David the great psalmist declared, saying, "I was formed in iniquity, and in sin my mother conceived me."[170,171]

St. Gregory of Nyssa says:

For You verily, O Lord, are the pure and eternal fount of goodness, Who did justly turn away from us, and in loving kindness did have mercy upon us. You did hate, and were reconciled; You did curse, and did bless; You did banish us from Paradise, and did recall us; You did strip off the fig-tree leaves, an unseemly covering, and put upon us a costly garment; You did open the prison, and did release the condemned; You did sprinkle us with clean water, and cleanse us from our filthiness. No longer shall Adam

---

(Washington, D.C.: The Catholic University of America Press, 1990), 223–224.

170 Cf. Psalms 51:5.
171 Cyril the Great, *Al-Sojoud Wa Al-Ibada Bi-Al Rouh Wa Al-Hak* [Worshipping and Serving in Spirit and in Truth], G.A. Ibrahim, trans. (Egypt: The Orthodox Center for Patristic Studies, 2017), 613. [Translated from Arabic text].

be confounded when called by You, nor hide himself, convicted by his conscience, cowering in the thicket of Paradise. Nor shall the flaming sword encircle Paradise around, and make the entrance inaccessible to those that draw near; but all is turned to joy for us that were the heirs of sin: Paradise, yea, heaven itself may be trodden by man: and the creation, in the world and above the world, that once was at variance with itself, is knit together in friendship: and we men are made to join in the angels' song, offering the worship of their praise to God.[172]

St. Severus of Antioch says:

Let us see how Peter and John and the rest of the Apostles raised up the church according to the likeness of this lame man[173], for she used to limp of old, like him, in the knowledge of God. And from her mother's womb she became paralyzed by sin because of the transgression of Adam and Eve, and she used to say, Behold I was formed in iniquity, and in sin my mother conceived me.[174] What did Peter and John, then, say to her when she was limping and yet she

---

172 Gregory of Nyssa *On the Baptism of Christ* (NPNF² 5:524).
173 See Acts 3.
174 Cf. Psalm 51:5.

asked for alms? They said, "Look at us."[175] With regards to teachings and health which streamed from her, and the new uprightness, the holy Apostles say that it is sufficient for you to only look at us.[176]

He also said:

How do I speak with tears? How do I show to you the grossness of sin? After He brought us out of nothing into existence, and gave us the honor of having authority over the beasts, birds, animals, and the whole earth, even that the beasts used to serve us [and were] subject to us, and the bear and wolf bore peace toward man, therefore, let the beasts themselves persuade you, for they were like the rest of the herd of the animals of pasture, gathering around Adam; when he gave them names in a special manner, he distinguished each kind by its name. But now after this authority was taken away from us because of sin, we no longer carry in ourselves the pure trait which is of the Divine image. For we fear the cruelty of ferocious beasts. We remember our ancient authority, so we

---

175 Acts 3:4.
176 M. Briere, *Les Homiliae Cathedrales de Severe d'Antioche: Homelies LXX a LXXVI*. (Paris, France: Firmin-Didot, 1915), 103. [Translated from Arabic text].

discover the sin of our race.[177]

Truly, we are born with a nature that is fallen, sinful, dead, corrupt, because of Adam's fall, sin and death. And we need to unite with Christ in Baptism; that we may receive in Him righteousness, and life, and resurrection, and incorruptibility.

"For all have sinned and fall short of the glory of God, being justified freely by His grace through the redemption that is in Christ Jesus."[178] All, here, including children.

> What then? Are we better than they? Not at all. For we have previously charged both Jews and Greeks that they are all under sin. As it is written: "There is none righteous, no, not one; there is none who understands; there is none who seeks after God. They have all turned aside; they have together become unprofitable; there is none who does good, no, not one."[179]

Therefore, we pray in the rite of Baptism, for children also, "Grant them the forgiveness of their sins, and grant them by Your grace that they may be healed from the destroying sin."[180]

---

177 Ibid.
178 Romans 3:23–24.
179 Romans 3:9–12.
180 Rite of Holy Baptism for Children – Litany.

And we confess in our prayers the existence of the defilement of sin in us all, without exception, "For You know, as creator of our being, that no one born of a woman shall be justified before You."[181]

"For no one is pure and without blemish, even though his life on earth be a single day."[182]

Therefore, Baptism according to the Orthodox Creed is for the remission of sins, and it did not say, "We believe in one baptism to heal the corrupt nature," though we actually believe that it is for the remission of sins, healing of the corrupt nature, obtaining of eternal life, becoming members of the Body of Christ[183], receiving adoption by God the Father, and restoring the image of God in man. Therefore, it is evident then that the Fathers of the Council of Constantinople, when they formulated this part of the Creed, knew that it is not possible to treat the side effects, without treating the root of the disease. For we cannot receive all these gifts through Baptism, without the remission of sin first.

Sin and its Consequences

Sin cannot be separated from its consequences, such that we talk about the inheritance of death and corruption, [yet] ignoring the original germ (sin), as these who deny the inheritance of sin teach.

---

181 Prayer of Reconciliation of St. Severus of Antioch.
182 Litany of the Departed.
183 Literally: sharing in the membership of the Body of Christ.

"For the law of the Spirit of life in Christ Jesus has made me free from the law of sin and death."[184]

The skilled physician does not treat the symptoms of the disease, but its root, and this is what the true Physician of our souls did with us.

St. Cyril the Great says:

But when the Savior says to him, "Man, your sins are forgiven," He addresses this generally to mankind: for those who believe in Him, being healed of the diseases of the soul, will receive forgiveness of the sins which formerly they had committed. Or He may mean this; I must heal your soul before I heal your body: for if this be not done, by obtaining strength to walk, you do but sin the more: and even though you have not asked for this, yet I as God see the maladies of the soul, which brought upon you this disease.... And when he was in the presence of Him Who is able to heal, his faith was accepted: and that faith can take away sin, Christ immediately shows; for He proclaims to him as he lay there, "Your sins are forgiven".... Well, therefore, does Christ announce that He will cut away the cause of the disease, and the very root, as it were, of the malady, even sin: for if this be removed, necessarily must the disease which sprung

---
184 Romans 8:2.

from it be also at the same time taken away.[185]

Once again **St. Cyril the Great** explains and teaches the same teaching:

> Why does his [Adam's] fall affect us? Why have we been condemned with him when we were not even born yet? On the contrary, God says, "Fathers will not be put to death for their children," nor children for their fathers, and, "It is the soul who sins that shall die."[186] What defense could we make for our position? It is indeed the soul who sins that shall die. Nevertheless, we have become sinners through Adam's disobedience in the following way.... When he [Adam] fell under sin, however, and sank into decay, then pleasures and impurities rushed into the nature of the flesh, and a savage law sprang up in our members. So our nature contracted sin "through the disobedience of the one man" (that is, Adam). That is how "the many were made sinners"[187]—not because they transgressed along with Adam (since they did not yet exist), but because they were of his nature,

---

[185] Cyril of Alexandria, *A Commentary upon the Gospel According to S. Luke* 1, R.P. Smith, trans. (Oxford, ENG: Oxford Press, 1859), 81–82.
[186] Deuteronomy 24:16.
[187] Romans 5:19.

which had fallen under the law of sin. Just as human nature was enfeebled with decay in Adam through his disobedience (and that is how the passions entered into it), so also it has been freed once again in Christ. He was obedient to God the Father and "committed no sin."[188,189]

The Biological, Genetic Aspect [of Sin]

The inheritance of sin, death and corruption should not be understood biologically and genetically; likewise, we should not explain our receiving the inheritance of salvation and eternal life in a biological and genetic aspect, but in a true spiritual meaning. We believe that sin did not turn into a material part of our material human nature. For sin did not turn into genes and did not mix naturally with human matter, [that] we then inherited this human, material, organic part, that is, sin; no, we believe, very simply, that we sinned in Adam when he sinned, because we were in his loins, and God judged all with the sentence of death in Adam.

St. Athanasius the Apostolic says, "Since every man is under sentence of death, according to what

---

[188] 1 Peter 2:22.

[189] Cyril of Alexandria, *Commentaries on Romans, 1-2 Corinthians, and Hebrews*, J.C. Elowsky, G.L. Bray, M. Glerup, and T.C. Oden, eds.; D.R. Maxwell, trans. (Downers Grove, IL: IVP Academic, 2022), 6–7.

was said to all in Adam, 'earth you are and unto earth you shall return.'"[190]

St. Cyril the Great says:

Cyril: Do you not accept, my dear [friend], that human nature became guilty to death because of that ancient curse? For it was previously said to us in the beginning of our race and in our first root, that is, Adam, "For dust you are, and to dust you shall return."[191]

Palladius: I, of course, accept this.[192]

For we were in Adam when he sinned, so his sin and its consequences cleaved to us, according to the expression of **St. Cyril the Great**:

He was scourged unjustly, that He might deliver us from merited chastisement; He was buffeted and smitten, that we might buffet Satan, who had buffeted us, and that we might escape from the sin that cleaves to us through the original transgression. For if we think aright, we shall believe that all Christ's sufferings were for us and on our

---

190 Athanasius *Letters of Athanasius* 61.3 (NPNF[2] 4:579).
191 Genesis 3:19.
192 Cyril the Great, *Al-Sojoud Wa Al-Ibada Bi-Al Rouh Wa Al-Hak* [Worshipping and Serving in Spirit and in Truth], G.A. Ibrahim, trans. (Egypt: The Orthodox Center for Patristic Studies, 2017), 104. [Translated from Arabic text].

behalf, and have power to release and deliver us from all those calamities we have deserved for our revolt from God.[193]

And as Adam's sin cleaved to us without genetic, biological explanation, so are we justified through the righteousness of Christ, and we live through His life, without any genetic, biological explanation.

"For as by one man's disobedience many were made sinners, so also by one Man's obedience many will be made righteous."[194]

St. Cyril the Great says:

For the whole nature of man became guilty in the person of him who was first formed [Adam]; but now it is wholly justified again in Christ.[195]

For sin is not something material, and neither are righteousness, death, and life. Therefore, inheritance here is not understood with a biological, genetic view, neither in the case of sin, nor of righteousness.

"And if [we are] children, then heirs—heirs of

---

193 Cyril of Alexandria, *Commentary on the Gospel according to S. John* 2. (London, ENG: Walter Smith, 1885), 606.

194 Romans 5:19.

195 Cyril of Alexandria, *A Commentary upon the Gospel According to S. Luke* 1, R.P. Smith, trans. (Oxford, ENG: Oxford Press, 1859), 171.

God and joint heirs with Christ."[196]

And it is possible for a person to inherit from their father a huge fortune, possessions, and property, and this has no genetic, biological aspect to it. And it is likewise possible for a person to inherit from their father many debts, and without any biological, genetic explanation too.

Why did the Fathers Focus on the Inheritance of Death and Corruption?

That some of the sayings of the Fathers and the liturgical texts focus on the inheritance of death and corruption "φθορά" more than focusing on the inheritance of Original Sin, does not mean that they do not approve the inheritance of sin. And this could happen in all the teaching of the Church. For example, in the Creed, it is said, "He suffered, was buried, and rose," so does this mean, because it did not say, "He suffered, died, was buried, and rose," that the Creed has denied the death of the Lord?

Likewise, in the Creed of Nicea and Constantinople, there is no mention of the Eucharist, nor the Priesthood, nor the prayer for the departed, nor the intercessions of the saints—does this indicate that the Fathers did not approve of these doctrines?

On the contrary, sometimes not mentioning

---

196 Romans 8:17.

a subject, or not focusing on it, is a proof that there is no second view about it. In [the Council of] Nicea they did not talk about the divinity of the Holy Spirit, and in the Nicene Creed nothing was mentioned about the Holy Spirit, because the matter of His divinity was not a subject of doubt or examination.

If someone found one of the esteemed Church Fathers, who does not approve of the inheritance of Adam's sin in some explicit texts, these writings must be understood [to mean] that we did not partake in the [act of] eating with Adam as individuals who are born and distinct from him, because we did not exist yet as individuals descending from Adam. This is exactly what our Church believes in, formerly and currently.

We must study the circumstances in which the [Church] Father explains the faith. For some of the Fathers were facing the heresy of Mani which prohibited marriage, and [taught] that sin became mingled with human nature, as though it had a material entity. Of this the Church does not agree, formerly and currently.

And perhaps it was this heresy which our teacher Paul the Apostle pointed to, in his epistle to his disciple Timothy:

> Now the Spirit expressly says that in latter times some will depart from the faith, giving heed to deceiving spirits and doctrines of

demons, speaking lies in hypocrisy, having their own conscience seared with a hot iron, forbidding to marry, and commanding to abstain from foods which God created to be received with thanksgiving by those who believe and know the truth.[197]

In Christ we are Justified by Grace

And as in Adam we became sinners before we existed as individuals, and without partaking with him in the [act of] eating, therefore, likewise also, without any merit on our part, we receive the righteousness of Christ, and His victory over death, and the outpouring of His life into us; and this is through faith in Him, then [through] uniting with Him in Baptism and the Eucharist.

When we are united with Christ, the Bridegroom of the soul, we become in Him righteous through His righteousness, and living through His life, and incorruptible through His eternal life which is poured out into us; with the necessity of persistence in our uniting with Him until the end, through our Church life which includes continual repentance, prayer, and spiritual struggle in Christ.

The Lord Christ has treated what previously afflicted our humanity in Adam.

St. John Chrysostom says:

---

[197] 1 Timothy 4:1–3.

How did it [death] reign? "After the similitude of Adam's transgression, who is the figure of Him that was to come." Now this is why Adam is a type of Christ. How a type? it will be said. Why in that, as the former became to those who were sprung from him, although they had not eaten of the tree, the cause of that death which by his [Adam's] eating was introduced; thus also did Christ become to those sprung from Him, even though they had not wrought righteousness, the Provider of that righteousness which through His Cross He graciously bestowed on us all.[198]

Knowing that we now enjoy the remission of sins as the most important blessing of the blessings of the incarnation and redemption; as to receiving life and incorruptibility, they are now a pledge, but they will be in truth in the blissful eternity.

✤ "For as in Adam all die, even so in Christ all shall be made alive. But each one in his own order: Christ the firstfruits, afterword those who are Christ's at His coming."[199]

✤ "So also is the resurrection of the dead. The body is sown in corruption, it is raised in incorruption."[200]

---

198 John Chrysostom *Homilies on the Epistle of St. Paul the Apostle to the Romans* 10 (NPNF[1] 11:402).
199 1 Corinthians 15:22–23.
200 1 Corinthians 15:42.

✣ "Now this I say, brethren, that flesh and blood cannot inherit the kingdom of God; nor does corruption inherit incorruption."[201]

✣ "In a moment, in the twinkling of an eye, at the last trumpet. For the trumpet will sound, and the dead will be raised incorruptible, and we shall be changed. For this corruptible must put on incorruption, and this mortal must put on immortality. So when this corruptible has put on incorruption, and this mortal has put on immortality, then shall be brought to pass the saying that is written: 'Death is swallowed up in victory.'"[202]

✣ "Blessed and holy is he who has part in the first resurrection. Over such the second death has no power, but they shall be priests of God and of Christ, and shall reign with Him a thousand years."[203]

The first resurrection is Baptism and repentance; as to the second resurrection, it is the promise we were promised in Christ Jesus our Lord, which is the resurrection of the body and incorruptibility.

✣ "And this is the promise that He has promised us—eternal life."[204]

This promise the Lord Jesus declared repeatedly

---

201 1 Corinthians 15:50.
202 1 Corinthians 15:52–54.
203 Revelation 20:6.
204 1 John 2:25.

in [the Gospel of] John chapter six, "I will raise him up at the last day."

✢ "This is the will of the Father who sent Me, that of all He has given Me I should lose nothing, but should raise it up at the last day. And this is the will of Him who sent Me, that everyone who sees the Son and believes in Him may have eternal life; and I will raise him up at the last day."[205]

✢ "No one can come to Me unless the Father who sent Me draws him; and I will raise him up at the last day."[206]

✢ "Whoever eats My flesh and drinks My blood has eternal life, and I will raise him up at the last day."[207]

St. Cyril the Great says:

> In order that He might expiate the guilt of Adam's transgression, He showed Himself obedient and submissive in every respect to God the Father in our stead: for it is written, "That as through the disobedience of the One man, the many were made sinners, so also through the obedience of the One, the many shall be made just" (Romans 5:19).[208]

---

205 John 6:39–40.

206 John 6:44.

207 John 6:54.

208 Cyril of Alexandria, *A Commentary upon the Gospel According to S. Luke* 1, R.P. Smith, trans. (Oxford, ENG: Oxford Press, 1859), 19.

St. Athanasius the Apostolic says:

That, since all were under sentence of death, He, being other than them all, might Himself for all offer to death His own body; and that henceforth, as if all had died through Him, the word of that sentence might be accomplished (for "all died" in Christ), and all through Him might thereupon become free from sin and from the curse which came upon it.[209]

Therefore, let us rejoice in what Christ has done for us, and not waste our life in debates that do not edify.

And this is what our teacher Paul the Apostle meant by his saying, "who is a type of Him who was to come."[210] For Adam is a type of Christ "who was to come;" therefore, what happened to us in Adam is repaired for us in Christ.

If we do not believe that we became sinners in Adam without partaking with him in the eating, according to the manner I have previously explained, so how do we accept that we are justified in Christ without any merit on our part?

God the Word was incarnate to save us from this bad state (sin, death and corruption).

---

209 Athanasius *Four Discourses Against the Arians* 2.21.69 (NPNF[2] 4:386).
210 Romans 5:14.

The Issue of the Sin of our Father Adam

For many contracted the sin of Adam, and many receive the righteousness of Christ. And the comparison between our contracting Adam's sin with our receiving Christ's righteousness is distinct from the comparison between the death which we suffered as a result of Adam's sin and eternal life which we receive in Christ Jesus our Lord, as it came in the first epistle to the Corinthians, "for since by man came death, by Man also came the resurrection of the dead. For as in Adam all die, even so in Christ all shall be made alive."[211]

St. Cyril the Great says:

He tasted death upon the tree and the cross, that He might take away from the midst the offence incurred by reason of the tree (of knowledge), and abolish the guilt that was thereby, and strip death of his tyranny over us. We have seen Satan fall: that cruel one broken: that haughty one laid low: him who had made the world submit to the yoke of His empire, stripped of his dominion over us.[212]

He also says:

He abolished sin which is the cause of the corruption that entered into us. And

---

211 1 Corinthians 15:21–22.

212 Cyril of Alexandria, *A Commentary upon the Gospel According to S. Luke* 1, R.P. Smith, trans. (Oxford, ENG: Oxford Press, 1859), 308.

if sin is abolished, then the stripes and punishments, which result from it, are inevitably abolished.[213]

St. John Chrysostom says:

After that he shows that it was not that sin only that was done away by the grace, but all the rest too, and that it was not that the sins were done away only, but that righteousness was given. And Christ did not merely do the same amount of good that Adam did of harm, but far more and greater good. Since then he had made such declarations as these, he wants again here also further confirmation of these. And how does he give this confirmation? He says, "For if by one man's offence death reigned by one, much more they which receive abundance of grace and of the gift of righteousness shall reign in life by one, Jesus Christ."[214] What he says, amounts to this nearly. What armed death against the world? The one man's eating from the tree only. If then death attained so great power from one offence, when it is found that certain received a grace and

---

213 Cyril the Great, *Al-Sojoud Wa Al-Ibada Bi-Al Rouh Wa Al-Hak* [Worshipping and Serving in Spirit and in Truth], G.A. Ibrahim, trans. (Egypt: The Orthodox Center for Patristic Studies, 2017), 326. [Translated from Arabic text].
214 Romans 5:17.

righteousness out of all proportion to that sin, how shall they still be liable to death? And for this cause, he does not here say "grace," but "superabundance of grace." For it was not as much as we must have to do away the sin only, that we received of His grace, but even far more.[215]

St. Ephraim the Syrian says, "Sin enslaved all bodies, but by one body without iniquity, grace liberated every body."[216]

St. Cyril the Great says:

For the whole nature of man became guilty in the person of him who was first formed [Adam]; but now it is wholly justified again in Christ. For He became for us the second commencement of our race after that primary one.[217]

He also says:

It was the Only-begotten Word of God, by submitting Himself to our estate, and being

---

215 John Chrysostom *Homilies on the Epistle of St. Paul the Apostle to the Romans* 10 (NPNF[1] 11:402–403).

216 St. Ephraim the Syrian, *Fi Al-Kanisa aw Al-Jihad Al-Masihi* [On the Church or the Christian Struggle], Bolous Al-Faghali, trans. (Beirut, Lebanon: *Al-Jami'ah Al-Antoniea*, 2006) 102. [Translated from Arabic text].

217 Cyril of Alexandria, *A Commentary upon the Gospel According to S. Luke* 1, R.P. Smith, trans. (Oxford, ENG: Oxford Press, 1859), 171.

found in fashion as a man, and becoming obedient unto the Father even unto death. Thus has the guilt of the disobedience that is by Adam been remitted: thus has the power of the curse ceased, and the dominion of death been brought to decay. And this too Paul teaches, saying "For as by the disobedience of the one man, the many became sinners, so by the obedience of the One, the many became righteous."[218,219]

St. Gregory of Nyssa says:

For as they who owing to some act of treachery have taken poison, allay its deadly influence by means of some other drug (for it is necessary that the antidote should enter the human vitals in the same way as the deadly poison, in order to secure, through them, that the effect of the remedy may be distributed through the entire system), in like manner we, who have tasted the solvent of our nature [that is, the forbidden fruit], necessarily need something that may combine what has been so dissolved, so that such an antidote entering within us may, by its own counter-influence, undo the mischief introduced into the body by

---

218 Romans 5:19.
219 Cyril of Alexandria, *A Commentary upon the Gospel According to S. Luke* 1, R.P. Smith, trans. (Oxford, ENG: Oxford Press, 1859), 171.

the poison. What, then, is this remedy to be? Nothing else than that very Body which has been shown to be superior to death, and has been the First-fruits of our life. For, in the manner that, as the Apostle says[220], a little leaven assimilates to itself the whole lump, so in like manner that body to which immortality has been given it by God, when it is in ours, translates and transmutes the whole into itself. For as by the admixture of a poisonous liquid with a wholesome one the whole draught is deprived of its deadly effect, so too the immortal Body, by being within that which receives it, changes the whole to its own nature.[221]

It should be noted that, in this text, St. Gregory of Nyssa confirms that we ate in Adam, thereby the dissolution of our nature occurred, and that the antidote of immortality is the partaking[222] of the body of the Lord, as a treatment for our nature which died in Adam.

I Believe That the Christian Faith is Summarized in the Following Truths:

1. We were created in Adam, and Adam was

---

220 1 Corinthians 5:6.
221 Gregory of Nyssa *The Great Catechism* 37 (NPNF² 5:504–505).
222 Literally: eating.

supposed to preserve the oneness of the human race in him, considering that he is the one head of the one humankind. (The oneness of the human race).

2. Adam's fall and his disobedience made the entire human race sinful in him, and guilty, dead, and corrupt.

3. There had to be a new head for humankind, to gather them in Himself and to grant them eternal life. And there is no one worthy of assuming this role, except the Logos, the Son of the Father, who is above all.

4. Therefore, the Logos took a body, fully equal to us, except for sin alone. He took it from a pure Virgin without the seed of man, that He may be a new head for a new humankind.

5. And in this, His own body, the Lord Jesus lived as a perfect man, and tasted death on behalf of all, and trampled on death, humiliated and abolished it, through the resurrection from among the dead, as a firstborn of those who have fallen asleep.

6. There is an opportunity for every person, to be saved from sin, death, and corruption, which we suffered because of Adam. This opportunity is [acquired] through faith in Christ, and accepting Him, and uniting with Him, by Baptism and the Eucharist.

7. Through uniting with Christ, the only begotten Son, we become in Him and through Him

children of God the Father, and we receive in Him and through Him righteousness, resurrection, and eternal life.

8. In our life on earth, we receive adoption by God the Father, and put on the righteousness of Christ, and are a temple of the Holy Spirit.

9. The person who stands fast to the end in Christ receives in Him and through Him resurrection, eternal life, eternal glory, and sitting with Him on His throne, in the blissful eternity.

This is the faith of our Church which we received from our Fathers; and those who have another opinion which is their own, let them, of course, discuss [it] in a scholarly way, within the limits of theological institutes, and with love, far from confusing the people.